MY NAME IS AMRITA...

born to be an artist

Anjali Raghbeer
inspired by the diaries of young Amrita

Tulika

Amrita on the right with her sister Indira on the left

Nine-year-old Amrita

My name is Amrita.
My father is Sikh and mother Hungarian.
That makes my sister and me
half Hungarian and half Indian.
I call my father Apuka, and my mother Anyuka.

These are Amrita's diaries. The first one (bottom left) was given to her as a Christmas present by her Uncle Ervin in 1920, when she was seven years old. She wrote in her diaries first in Hungarian and later in English, and filled them with sketches, stories, poems, her thoughts and feelings, everyday happenings and even historical events.

I am eight years old
and we have moved to India.

I miss Hungary.

Nobody speaks Hungarian
in India. When I miss home my
Anyuka tells me Hungarian stories.
The best ones she tells me are
about fairies.

I draw them in my book.

If I don't draw I can't sleep.

Amrita's childhood sketchbooks are full of colour pencil
drawings of Hungarian folk stories and fairytales. She
would also write and illustrate her own stories and poems.

Once upon a time there was a fairy and that fairy always wore a kind of peacock dress...

Once upon a time there was a fairy.
The little fairy always played...

Once upon a time there was a fairy queen and this fairy queen was always sad...

Anyuka tells me the story of the miracle tree. It goes like this –

Once upon a time there was a tree.
The tree had a young owner and that young owner
was always like that miracle tree.
Everybody called it the miracle tree because this tree
was such a tree that changed the colour of its flowers according
to the young owner.

Once blue,
once pink,
once green,
all kinds of colours.
But the scent was always that of lilac. And this tree was this
little girl's jewel and her mother was proud of her
and they lived happily ever after.

Anyuka had an idea that we should go to Italy.

She, Indu and I.

I don't want to go so far from India.
I've never been through such a sad day in my whole life as when we separated from our angel Apuka.
He was not even allowed on the ship to say 'see you' to us.
Oh, how my heart was aching.
I was 11 years old.

I am so miserable. *I miss my Apuka.*

My dear sweet dad,
please come as soon as possible.
Kissing you thousand times,
            your loving Amrita.

I would send you chocolate
if it would not melt.

I hate hate hate school in Italy.
Anyuka put us into a huge
elegant school but still very
nasty school,
its name is S. S. Annunciata.

Only 1 time in 1 year we and other children are allowed to be taken out.

On Sunday dear Anyuka will take us out for the whole day because that day will be Induska's birthday.

We get ready and wait for Anyuka.

Dressed in a cloak and hat, waiting for her mother – Amrita's drawing of herself in her diary.

Although she had been living in India from when she was eight, the people and sceneries in Amrita's paintings as a young girl were usually very European.

First we went to Palazzo Pitti. Everything is beautiful there.

And then to our house.
I am so happy today.
There were presents from our one and only Apuka.

I am on the ship going back to India, dear India, after many days. *The sun shines as fire.*

Simla is
hills, hills, hills and mountains.
I lay down on the short grass.
And looked up at the glorious
azure sky with a few diamond
stars which bespangled the vast
deep blueness of it.

1921.
Simla

Amrita's father, Sardar Umrao Singh Sher-Gil, loved photography and took many pictures of the family. These were taken in Simla between 1921 and 1928, and show Amrita with her father (in a turban, with and without a beard), her mother Marie Antoinette, and sister Indira.

*A draga angyal Mucika
a kényelmes karoszékiben
Amrita rajzolta
11 éves koraban Simla. 14. Junius 1924*

Simla is home because I am with Mummy…
She plays the piano magnificently.
She sings so well.
Her voice is like an organ in its deep tones.
She even knows Puccini,
the great Italian composer
who wrote Madame Butterfly.

Simla is home because I am with Indu…
My dear sister who is so musical too. And
always cheerful. She makes friends easily.
So so different from me.

And Daddy… He is not musical. He is
always reading serious books. Even if you
put his pugri upside down. He speaks
Sanskrit and Persian. And writes verses of
Omar Khayyam in beautiful letters. He
dresses like Tolstoy, the Russian writer.

Simla is friends…
Zoe,
Myra,
Esme,
Una.
And picnics…

Oh, and the best is I don't go to school, even though I am almost eleven. Not that Anyuka didn't try. But Mother Superior didn't think I should come to her school because I did not believe in God!

Fancy that!!!!

Amrita's Uncle Ervin came to Simla in 1926. Under his guidance, her lines became stronger and more angular. She has done many self-portraits. This is one of her early ones.

So now I study at home. It's much
better that way because I learn lots of
things.

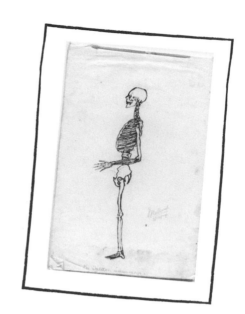

Music.
Bach, Chopin (Indu likes him but isn't he too sentimental?),
Tchaikovsky, Nicolai Rimsky Korsakov, and my favourite Beethoven.

Tchaikovsky's Serenade Melancolique…
the sadness, the passion, tear your soul out.

Amrita's sketch of the composer Beethoven,
whom she admired. She would often quote
what he is believed to have said about
refusing to bow before Napoleon: 'There will
be many emperors but only one Beethoven.'

Dance.

Theatre.

Many of Amrita's early paintings were emotional scenes from films and books.
She won her first prize for art for one such piece when she was ten, a cash award of 50 rupees.

And… painting. It is my shadow, always with me.

As a little girl, Amrita passionately painted the fairytales she heard. As she grew older, the films she saw and book she read were all subject matter for her paintings, especially women characters from them. The music of great composers like Beethoven, Chopin and Tchaikovsky also had a strong influence on her art when she was young.

Sometimes I think when I grow up, I'll be an artist because that's what I like doing best.

Amrita once went for a wedding where the bride was thirteen years old, about her own age at that time. This is the picture she painted of the bride. She also wrote about how sad and lonely the girl looked. Even later, she liked to paint what people were thinking.

Or maybe a musician. Anyuka would really like that.

I think I am a philosopher because
*I work out the remotest depths of my extraordinary
ideas. Philosophers usually work out their thoughts till they
get the conclusion of their idea.*

I have turned thirteen. I feel all grown up. I draw what I feel. Sometimes dark pictures when I'm angry. Bliss…

These days I like to draw the silent movies (which I am allowed to go and watch!). Betty Blythe in 'Queen of Sheba'. Rudolph Valentino in 'The Sheik'. He takes your breath away. Conrad Viedt. Countess Rina de Liguoro in 'Savitri'. Ramon Novarro in 'Prisoner of Zenda'. Could anyone be more handsome?

Sketches made by Amrita in her diary after seeing films or reading books. She would think about the characters afterwards and sketch them. She made a list of all her favourite films in her diary.

Uncle Ervin has arrived from Hungary. He is simply wonderful. He teaches me to draw from live models and is very impressed with my drawings. He says I should go to Paris.

Paris? Art capital of the world? Mummy would like that. Indu can learn the piano better there. But Daddy is not keen.

What do I want?

Daddy is convinced (thanks to
Uncle Ervin). The ship sails for Paris.

École Nationale des Beaux Arts.
Just thinking of it gives me goosebumps.

I am sixteen.
My journey begins.

The journey to which I was born … to be an artist.

Looking at Amrita Sher-Gil's paintings

From the time Amrita was a little girl growing up in the Hungarian countryside, she loved to draw the colours and shapes around that fascinated her. She drew on the walls or on any bit of paper that she could find. Her drawings, as much as her writings, tell us about her thoughts and feelings as she was growing up.

Amrita was born into a family that was able to give her the best education, whether in art or music, and to support her desire to be an artist. She was lucky to have travelled, even as a child, to the great centres of Western art like Paris and Florence, where she could see the work of famous painters.

Boat, 1932, Hungary

Notre Dame, 1932, Paris

Hungarian Village Church, 1932, Hungary

Her uncle Ervin Baktay, who was himself an artist and came to Simla in 1926, played a very important role in guiding her. He encouraged her to go to Paris to study art when she was 16. She took a degree at the well-known art school, École Nationale des Beaux Arts, studying under Lucien Simon till 1932. She then set up her own studio and tried to paint in the style of European painters such as Cezanne, Gauguin, Modigliani, and others. From Paris, she would go every year to Hungary and spend several months there. But the Indian side of her identity kept expressing itself – in her art, in the way she dressed, and finally in her craving to come back.

Self-Portrait (7), 1930, Paris

Young Man With Apples, 1932, Paris

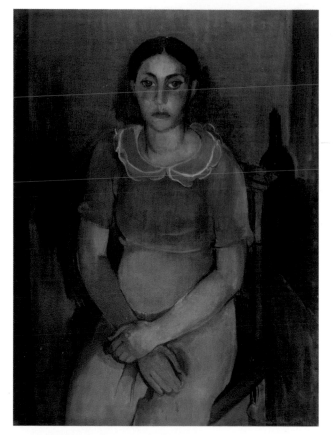

Study of Model (2), 1934, Paris

"I began to be haunted by an intense longing to return to India," Amrita wrote, "feeling in some strange inexplicable way that there lay my destiny as a painter." She came back to India in 1934, and from then on began to explore Indian art traditions. She travelled widely through villages and did many paintings of villagers and village life. In *Group of Three Girls*, one of her earliest well-known paintings, we can see how she began to move away from the realistic style she had learnt to a flatter, modern approach. It shows three young women with sad expressions. This look was typical of many of the women in her paintings, like some of the others seen here. There is an air of dignity as well as sadness about them, almost as if the artist can see into their minds and understand their thoughts and feelings, as with the child bride years ago. During her earlier years in India, the people in Amrita's paintings had looked very European. Now, to show India and ordinary Indian people she changed her Western way of painting to use richer, more vibrant tones.

Group of Three Girls, 1935, Amritsar

Hill Women, 1935, Simla

Hill Men, 1935, Simla

Brahmacharis, 1937, Simla

South Indian Villagers Going to Market, 1937, Simla

Bride's Toilet, 1937, Simla

Bride, 1940, Saraya

The Ajanta caves inspired her strong use of white, and brought in a certain spiritual quality. She was dazzled by the brilliant colours and details of miniature paintings introduced to her by art historian and critic Karl Khandalavala. Her journey through the southern parts of the subcontinent resulted in the famous South Indian trilogy – *Brahmacharis, Bride's Toilet,* and *South Indian Villagers going to Market*.

Amrita married her cousin, Victor Egan, in Budapest in 1938. They came to live in India, and spent two years on her uncle's estates in Saraya, near Gorakhpur, where she painted most of her important works of this period. They moved to Lahore in 1941. It was here that she did her last piece, a view from her studio window, for she died of an illness three months after going there. She was then only 28 years old – so young, but already a pioneer of modern art in India.

To Urvi and Udita, who might find their creative space some day – AR

The Looking at Art series:
My Name is Amrita – *Amrita Sher-Gil, painter*
A Trail of Paint – *Jamini Roy, painter*
The Veena Player – *Ravi Varma, painter*
Barefoot Husain – *M. F. Husain, painter*

My name is Amrita... born to be an artist (English)
ISBN 978-81-8146-653-2
© *story* Anjali Raghbeer
First published in India, 2009
Reprinted in 2011, 2017

Design: Radhika Menon

*Our deepest thanks to Vivan Sundaram for his help and cooperation, and to Vivan and Navina Sundaram
for permission to reproduce Amrita Sher-Gil's paintings, drawings and photographs from their collection,
and to use extracts from her childhood diaries, in this book.*

Courtesy National Gallery of Modern Art, New Delhi: Camels, Notre Dame, Boat, Young Man With Apples,
Study of Model (2), Self Portrait (7), Group of Three Girls, Brahmacharis, Bride's Toilet, Bride

Published by
Tulika Publishers, 24/1 Ganapathy Colony Third Street Teynampet, Chennai 600 018, India
email reachus@tulikabooks.com website www.tulikabooks.com

Printed and bound by
Sterling and Quadra Press India Limited, #710, Anna Salai, Nandanam, Chennai 600 035, India